Gloria

The story of two brothers' journey into

the world of rock and roll, and

how it affected their lives.

Gloria

The story of two brothers' journey into
the world of rock and roll, and
how it affected their lives.

By Charlie Bartolomeo

ISBN: 9781079149661

Cover design by TeaBerryCreative.com

Dedication

I dedicate this book to my wife, Laurel, our children, Elizabeth and Christopher, and to Suzy, Peter's wife, and their children, Matthew and Corina.

In memory of Gino Peter Bartolomeo, 1953-2018

"Finally, the story is going to be told!"

Table of Contents

Preface

When you meet someone and you find out they are also a musician, most people would feel a kinship of sorts with that person, even if you don't play the same music or instrument. I feel that everyone we meet in life has some kind of effect on our life, be it however so small. Well, in this book there are a lot of people mentioned who did just that, as well as many more people who weren't mentioned but still influenced our musical journey. For that, I would like to thank all of you on behalf of my late brother, Peter, and myself for touching our lives. Some of you only played a song with us; others may have played a number of times with us. Either way, it was always appreciated by Peter and me. So, thank you all again for the time we spent together playing and enjoying music.

Chapter One

The Country Boys

Let me begin with some family background. Peter and I grew up in a small town in the Hudson Valley in upstate New York. The town, Pine Plains, was typical of most small towns in America: one traffic light, two state roads that intersected, and some small businesses.

Peter was the youngest in our family of eight children; I was the next youngest. My mother and father moved up to Pine Plains from the Bronx in the summer of 1948. At that time they had five children. My brother Joe was the eldest, then came Richard, Francis, Robert and my only sister, Celia. My next older brother, Bill, was born in 1950, I was born in 1951, and Peter was born in 1953. Bill, Peter and I were known as the "country boys" because we were born after the move from the city. The age difference between Joe and Peter was 19 years.

Our mother, Rose, was the eldest of eight children. She helped raise her siblings, and then had eight of her own. Our mother was the best in the world. Our dad came to America from Poggio Sannita, Italy, in 1926 at the age of 18. His dad was here already and had served in the U.S. Army. Our father was one of the hardest working men I've ever met. In his lifetime he started and built three businesses. At some point, each of us children worked in one or more of the businesses.

Our family never took vacations, but we always had what we needed, we never went without, and we had an abundance of love for each other.

Standing: Dick, Joe and Fran
Seated: Celia, Rose pregnant with Peter and holding me,
Frank with Billy on lap and Bobby
Photo circa 1952

Chapter Two

Thank You, Mr. Foster

The school we attended was built in 1932, one of those massive three-story brick structures. On the first two floors were K through six and the top floor was the high school. Back then the music program began in sixth grade. It was a chorus class with Miss Johnston. It was an introductory class where we sang and learned the basics of music—whole notes, half notes, treble and bass clef, the scale. My friend Gary Keeler started drum lessons, aiming to be in the high school band. To make it into the band you had to start learning an instrument in the fifth or sixth grade.

Pine Plains Central School
Photo courtesy of Fred Couse

Our family was raised Roman Catholic, and Gary's family was also Catholic. We both ended up being altar boys later on. Back then, a lot of social things centered around the church. At Christmas that year we had ten days or two weeks off for vacation, and my mother and father had a party on New Year's Eve. A lot of the people from the church were there, and I remember staying up late and watching a movie, "The Tommy Dorsey Story." My friend Gary's parents were really into that Big-Band era sound, and I remember how neat it was watching this guy play the trombone. That was it; I was going to play the trombone!

When I got back to school after the Christmas holiday, I went right to Miss Johnston and told her I wanted to play the trombone and be in the band. She set it up so I could go see Mr. Foster up on the third floor in the band room. I remember going to the band room and the only people there were Mr. Foster and an older girl name Carol Hutzler, who was practicing her bass clarinet. Mr. Foster could be quite intimidating. He was an excellent trumpet player, was always neatly dressed, and he drove a Jaguar XKE. I told him I wanted to play trombone, so he said to me, "Do you know notes?" and I said, "Yes, I know whole notes, half notes, etc. etc." So then he gave me a trombone and told me to blow a "G." What proceeded for the next 30 or so minutes is the absolute truth! I kept saying the word "ghee" into the mouth piece, never even coming close to making any sound come out of that trombone! I remember Mr. Foster asking Carol to blow a G so I could hear it, and finally he took the trombone away and just gave me the mouthpiece to blow into. That didn't help either. I just kept blowing "ghee" into it. What seemed like an eternity finally came to an end as the period ended and band members started to come in. I told Mr. Foster that I didn't want to play the trombone, and he sent me back to Miss Johnston's class.

So that, boys and girls, is why I'm not a trombone player and again I say, "Thank you, Mr. Foster.

Mr. Foster (Play me a "G")

Chapter Three
Well, Hello Mr. Cohen!

After going through that experience back in sixth grade with Mr. Foster, I had to take a music appreciation course with him in 7th grade. We studied all the old classical composers. We had to listen to Bach, Beethoven, etc., and then write a composition on each one; it was boring. In 8th grade Miss Johnston left and was replaced by a young music teacher named Robert Cohen. Mr. Cohen was tall, had a bit of a temper, and really didn't put up with any crap. This was Fall 1964—things were kind of crazy back then. We had lost a president the year before, there was this war way over on the other side of the world, and in the U.S. there was a lot of division and strife. You have to remember, back then there was no internet, no cable TV, no cell phones, no Twitter, no SnapChat, no nothing. There were only three TV channels and we could get only two of them. One day in Mr. Cohen's class, he took out an acoustic guitar and started playing. That was it! I was hooked. He said he would give guitar lessons to anyone who wanted to learn.

I remember at that time my eldest brother Joe had a folk guitar. He had never learned to play it but still kept it, and my middle brother Bob had what he used to call "The Cowboy" guitar because it had black with white stenciled decorations on it. My little brother Peter was in 6th grade by then and he had classes with Mr. Cohen also. Peter and I decided to take lessons.

Now, back then the minimum wage was around $1.25 an hour. And if I remember correctly, Mr. Cohen charged Peter and me something like $3.00 or $4.00 for a lesson, and he took both of us at the same time. He introduced us to the guitar: the parts like bridge, nut frets, tuners, sound hole, and how to tune it; all the basics. He showed us various strums. We had a book with all the fingering positions for chords (open chords). He taught us songs that used these chords, like "Mr. Noah and "Oh, Mary". Peter and I would go home really excited and we practiced until the tips of our fingers bled, but we finally built up calluses on our fingertips. Later on, Peter and I would learn that on really good-quality guitars, the strings were easy to press down on the frets to make the sound. With the two guitars that Peter and I had then, the strings were so high off the fret board that we used to say "you could drive a Mack truck under them." But that is what we had. I sometimes wonder whether if Joe and Bob hadn't already had guitars, we would ever have been able to take lessons. So, Joe and Bob, thanks for letting us use them!

Things went along fairly smoothly. Peter and I always practiced together and sang those folk songs. In fact, I think my

Uncle Frank recorded us in my mother's living room once. I don't know if those tapes are still around somewhere. Uncle Frank's daughter, Maryanne, is keeping an eye out for them as she sorts through things in the family home.

Chapter Four

Sunday Nights Would Never Be the Same

We studied with Mr. Cohen for only 13 weeks. The thing that really ended our guitar lessons with him was a TV station out of Albany, NY, WRGB. They played the Ed Sullivan Show on Sunday nights, and that's where Peter and I saw the Beatles for the first time. February 9, 1964 changed it all.

Remember that I wrote that Mr. Cohen had a temper? Well, in our 13th week of lessons, Peter and I happened to mention to Mr. Cohen that we had seen the Beatles back in February 1964 and were now thinking about getting electric guitars so we could play rock and roll. Well, you would have thought that the world was coming to an end! He went ballistic, and we no longer took guitar lessons.

Mr. Cohen
(WHAT? You guys want to buy ELECTRIC guitars?)

By this time, Peter and I had established a solid practice routine. We would come home from school, change our clothes, do our homework, and then start practicing our guitars until it was supper time. As time went on and I was in ninth grade and Peter in seventh, I took an art class. I met a kid in art class, named Charlie Hanlon. He was older than Peter and me, and he had an electric guitar and amp. Long-story short, I bought the guitar and amp for, I think, $25.00. On Saturdays I had been working with my eldest brother, Joe, helping him with cleaning oil burners and making fuel oil deliveries, and I had saved some money and that's how the first electric guitar came to us.

The day I brought it home it was like Christmas for Peter and me. We went over this guitar with a fine-tooth comb. We took it totally apart just to see what was in there. The guitar was sunburst in color, with a single pickup. We took the pickguard off and saw all the wiring from the toggle switch to the pickup. To get the pickguard all the way off, we cut the wires. They were red, white and green. When we put it back together, we spliced the wires and soldered them and covered the connections with electrical tape. By now you're probably wondering, "Why is he telling us about the wires?" Well, this will prove to be very important later on in my story.

The room where we slept was quite large and originally there were four of us sleeping in there. But by now it was just Bill, Peter and me. Eventually Bill moved into another bedroom that had been vacated by our elder brother, Bob, who had gotten married. Now there were just Peter and me in this large bedroom. That meant we could keep our record player set up and leave the guitar and amp plugged in and ready to play. It was like having our own studio. Bob had a Duane Eddy album. It had "Rebel Rouser" on it. We also had a Beach Boys album we listened to. The amp that I got with the guitar was really small, with maybe an 8" speaker, but it had two inputs. I can't really remember how or when Peter got his first electric guitar, but it was robin's- egg blue and I think it was an Aria.

Now we were cooking: we wanted to play rock and roll. My parents knew a couple who had a weekend house on Twin Island Lake, Jim and Molly Amantia. Jim played the violin in the city. They would come over and play cards with my mother and father, and on one of those occasions, Jim showed Peter and me orchestra chords on our guitars. These looked really hard to play, or even learn how to play. But Peter and I were seeing all these rock groups on Sundays on the Ed Sullivan Show and they would be sliding their hands down the neck of the guitar and using their fingers as a capo. Once we were introduced to the bar chord, this became our next challenge: we had to learn how to master it.

Peter and I continued our practice routine. Somewhere in this time period, Peter picked up an amp. I think it was a Fender Princeton amp. Prior to that we had been playing out of the amp I got with my guitar, but with two guitars playing out of that little amp, we could get hardly any volume.

Chapter Five

Away in a Manger

The spring of 1965 was the first time Peter and I ever played music with anyone else. We had learned three or four songs by this time. The first one was "Gloria," a song by a group called Them. It was easy, just E, D, and A chords, all open chords just like we had learned from Mr. Cohen. All throughout our entire journey of playing rock and roll, we always seemed to start our sets with "Gloria." It was a good warm-up song. Actually, that song, "Gloria," has been covered more times than a potato salad at a 4th of July picnic. A lot of bands did versions of it.

I remember our first session during spring break. Three of Peter's school classmates came to our place to play. Two of them, John Boggs and Ray Najda, were from Elizaville, and Tommy Bauer was from Stanfordville. John sang. He had a mike and plugged into Ray's amp. Ray had a white Aria guitar just like Peter's. Tommy played the drums. The only place we could play was in our sheep shed/chicken coop; God's honest truth! The sheep were in a block building built onto the back of the old chicken coop. Pete and I had swept out the chicken coop (there weren't any chickens left). The chicken coop didn't have any electricity, so we ran an extension cord out the window of the two-car garage that my father had built with an apartment on top for my mother's parents in the '50s. The cord went across the lawn, through the grape arbor, through the wire fence, and across the sheep pasture to the coop. To this day, I still have that extension cord. Needless to say, I don't think anyone has ever heard "Gloria," "Louie, Louie," "Hang On Sloopy," and "House of the Rising Sun" with sheep on the other side of the wall singing "bah, bah, bah." So now you know why we only did this once, especially when our father found out.

The sheep shed/chicken coop where Peter and I started out

The next time we got together we played in a house our father had, just up the hill from our house. At the time, the house was empty so we could practice there. I think we only played there a couple of times. Years later I would buy this house from my mother, and Laurel and I raised our children there.

Peter and I began going to Kingston on Friday nights. Sometimes Gary would go with us. We would go to the Kingston Music Center, owned by two guys named Tony and Mike. They always treated us well, even though we were just school kids. Peter and I would look at all the guitars (Fender, Gibson, etc.) and we would drool. We would pick up brochures on everything, bring them home, and the pages would become dog-eared from our constantly looking through them.

In my art class that year there was a kid named Robert Krause. He was a pretty talented artist. I remember he made me a jade ring that I gave to my girl friend. Laurel still has that ring. Anyway, getting back to my story, Robert wanted to buy my electric guitar even though he didn't have an amp or know how to play, so I sold it to him and he kept it in the art room. The next time Peter and I went to Kingston to the music store, lo and behold, when we walked in we saw two knockoff Rickenbacker model 330 guitars hanging on the wall. They were sunburst red. And, you guessed it; we came home with these guitars. One was a 6-string which I bought, and Peter bought the 12-string. Pete traded his Aria in, and I used the money I got from Robert for my guitar and my savings to buy mine. We played these guitars through the early years in our first band called The Sole Distributor, but more on that later. For Peter and me, our next goal was to get better amps.

Peter bought an album by an instrumental group from the west coast. They were called The Ventures. The album was a double album with tablature inside (showing you how to finger the notes for the songs). One song on the album was "Walk Don't Run." Peter and I would come home from school and the moment we got to our bedroom, we would put the album on and play that song. Peter's son, Matthew, still has that album. If you play that album, it skips and jumps when you reach that song, because we literally wore the grooves out we played it so much. Peter and I played a lot of The Ventures hits. We really liked them.

As fate would have it, for Peter's 65th birthday (and it turned out to be his last), his son Matthew surprised Peter and, his wife, Suzy with dinner at a club where The Ventures were playing that night, and they dedicated "Sleepwalk" to Pete. On YouTube (The Ventures at Daryls House-Sleep Walk 2/26/18) you can see Peter's reaction. He gave them the thumbs up; you could tell he was overwhelmed and happy. Sadly, a little over a month later Peter would die.

Chapter Six
Classmates and The Sole Distributor

In the spring of the 1966 school year, Peter, Gary Keeler and I thought about forming a band. Gary and I were classmates of another fellow named Don Jett who lived in a town south of us called Bangall, which was part of Stanfordville. Gary played in the high school band with Don and we invited him to be our bass player. We kind of messed around off and on through the end of the school year and into the summer. Most of the time we got together at Gary's house for band practice. Thank God for Norma Keeler, Gary's mom! She would always encourage us and feed us lunch. As for Gary's dad, George, he would come home and we would be in the living room practicing. He would give us that look and just shake his head.

Horsing around at Gary's house

Me messing around with Don's
bass when practicing

Peter and me with our knock-off Rickenbacker guitars

Gary, Farley's girl friend, Linda, & me

Gary, me, Don with the hat
Peter and Farley in front

Band getting crazy

Gary keeping the beat

Herbie on the organ he built from a kit

Gary on the drums
(the best drummer we ever had)

Band's DayGlo® bass drum cover
designed and painted by Claudia Waag

Mr. Hyatt, our biology teacher,
who came up with our band's
name, The Sole Distributor

Gary's family spent a lot of time at the local town beach in the summer. My brothers Bill, Peter and I would go down after we finished our chores for the day. We used to see a man there a lot that we knew from my family's service station. He was a weekender and he would come into the station for gas or car service. Well, as it turned out, he was a composer. His name was Harold Selesky. We were told that he wrote the theme song for the 1964 World's Fair in NYC. Anyway, one day at the beach, we were talking with him and mentioned that we had formed a band. He said he had a friend who was a recording engineer and if we wanted, they would record us. Well, we were just high school kids and we were overwhelmed, but we jumped at the chance.

St. Anthony's Catholic Church

Photo courtesy of Jo Ann Keeler
St. Anthony's Catholic Church basement where
we made our first recording as a band.

Since we were altar boys, the priest, Father John, let us use the basement of St. Anthony's Church one Sunday afternoon to do the recording. Harold and his friend, Jerry Newman, recorded us on a big reel-to-reel tape recorder, and they said they would send us the finished product later. That was the second time Peter and I were ever recorded playing together, but this time it was as a band on electric guitars. Peter and I and the rest of the band thought we had made it. At that time we hadn't yet decided on a name for the band. Gary thought of JC and the Prophets or Prince and the Paupers. None of us really liked either of those, and we just kept practicing. That fall when school started, we had a biology teacher named Gary Hyatt. He was young, a real sharp dresser, and he had a sports car. Gary, Don and I were in his biology class. One day we were telling him about our band and when we said we didn't have a name yet, he suggested The Sole Distributor, and that's how we came up with the name.

I can't remember if it was before or after The Sole Distributor's first gig that we picked up another member, Farley Churton. He was a neighbor of Don's in Bangall and became our lead singer. We now had our Mick Jagger, so to speak. Our very first gig was at the house of Holly Adams, another classmate of ours. We got this gig through high jinx on the part of Gary and Don. Gary and Don played in the high school band with another classmate named Cindy Losee. She had a brother named Steve, who somehow magically became the manager of our band because Gary liked Cindy, and he set things up with Holly. Peter and I really didn't care; we just wanted to play rock and roll. Well, Steve got us that gig and another at a barn party in Ancramdale that one of the teachers, Mr. Clark, was having one weekend. So far The Sole Distributor had played in a living room and a barn. And, by the way, neither one were paid gigs.

Mr. Clark, who hosted our
Second gig at a barn party

Meanwhile, we were trying to build up our repertoire of songs to play. Most school dances were from 7:00 to 11:00 or 8:00 to 12:00. Even with breaks, we had to have enough songs to cover 3 hours. Don would say, "Oh, we've had requests for "House of the Rising Sun," or "Hey Joe," or "Tobacco Road." These were fairly long songs, so you could easily stretch them to get through the night.

Farley was the lead singer most of the time, Don sang lead occasionally, and Peter and I were just allowed to sing back-up. According to Don, we just didn't have the voices. Later in life, Don went on to become one of the top five Elvis impersonators in the U.S.A., so I guess he was probably right at that time. But to be fair, Don probably never heard Peter when he sang in Busted Out, another group we formed in the mid '70s, or much later, in the '90s, when Peter was in an a cappella group called The Gospel Truth. Peter had a larger range in his singing ability than I did, and I think that's why he did so well with the a cappella group. But I'm getting ahead of my story here.

Don Jett years later as
an Elvis impersonator

When Steve Losee got us that first gig at Holly's house, Peter and I were still using our little amps, but Don knew the guys at the Poughkeepsie Music Store, and I think he talked his mother, Matilda, into renting some amps for that gig. If I remember it right, the amps cost $25.00 for two days, and we rented a Gretsch bass amp and an Ampeg guitar amp. Needless to say, we only did that a couple of times until, as luck would have it, Peter and I ended up buying that used Ampeg Gemini VI for $100.00 from the music store. We pooled our money and finally had a big, powerful amp. Now we were on our way. The amp had echo, tremolo, and a 12" or 15" speaker. It was beautiful; we could both play out of it and still be heard.

As we got into '66-'67 school year, we started to play at school dances, usually every other Friday night. On alternate Fridays we would play in Bangall at St. Mary's Hall for their youth group. The whole band would go down immediately after school to set up the equipment and Mrs. Jett kindly fed us supper. Sometimes we would get as much as $30.00 or $40.00 from the class dances, though at St. Mary's, it was usually only $12.00 and a pizza. But we were playing as a group quite regularly and we enjoyed it.

St. Mary's Hall, Bangall, NY

Chapter Seven
The Art of Telling the Truth

Remember the kid from art class named Robert Krause who bought my old guitar? Well, one day I went to art class and found out that the guitar, which he used to keep in the art room had been stolen. I thought at the time it was strange. One Friday night after we had played at St Mary's Hall, we all went to a dance club called The Village Carousel in Stanfordville. They always had good bands and they usually had really nice equipment. Around that time a lot of the bands, including us, were into using strobe lights and DayGlo® paints. One guy was playing a 9-string guitar, all painted up. The guitar looked familiar to me and, sure enough, I recognized it as the old guitar that I had sold to Robert. I asked the kid where he had gotten the guitar and he told me the name of another kid who was in my art class. What happened next is what I would say is the "you-know-what hits the fan."

On Monday when I went back to school and got to art class, I told Robert the story and who the kid was who had taken his guitar. Now all hell broke loose. I had made an accusation of theft against a kid whose father was a teacher in our school. I was in the lunch room when the lunch room monitor, Mr. Schaehrer (the vocational agriculture teacher), called me aside and told me I had to go with him to the Principal's office because of the accusation I had made. Robert and the kid I accused of stealing the guitar and his father were waiting there. The Principal told me that I had made a serious charge. I told him that if they took the guitar apart they would see what colors the wires were, and how they were soldered together and covered with electrical tape. Mr. Schaehrer and I went down to the shop to get a screwdriver so I could remove the pickguard on the guitar.

What do you think happened? That's right; it was my old guitar. I can still remember how the kid who stole the guitar stammered and hemmed and hawed. His dad, the teacher, realized his son had stolen it and made him pay Robert $25.00 for the guitar. The Principal thanked me and gave me a "good job" wink. After that Peter and I always felt leery of the kid who had stolen that guitar. Later on we would run into him again on our journey playing music.

Chapter Eight

Rubbing Shoulders with Dean Martin and Jerry Lewis

Another thing that happened to us as a band affected all of us, even though we were in different grades. There were daily announcements over the PA system at school, about drama club meeting and other activities. In the early fall of 1966 we finally received the tape recording of the band that Harold and Jerry had made for us. Don, being the showman that he was, thought it would be a good idea to play the tape in the background of the daily announcement that informed everybody that The Sole Distributor was going to play for the upcoming school dance. We all thought this was a great idea until we realized we had never played the tape all the way through. Disaster struck that fateful day. Unbeknownst to us, Harold and Jerry had spliced some tape from the cutting room floor onto our songs. On the tape Dean Martin and Jerry Lewis were trying to do a promo of their movie "The Caddy." To this day I still don't know if it was jesting or real, but they used every curse word you could come up with against each other in the promo. When that came over the PA system at school, the you-know what hit the fan. Boy, did we get yelled at, especially Don himself, since he was in the Principal's office and running the tape during the announcements.

In October of 1966 Don got us a gig at a Halloween party in Hyde Park, N.Y. for some college kids. The guy who organized the party wanted us to play a certain song, during which he was going to propose to his girl. We played that song three times, and she turned him down every time. While we all thought that it was pretty funny at the time, I'm sure he didn't.

We played a lot through that school year. All that time Peter and I kept to our practice routine and we were getting more and more comfortable playing in front of people. A funny thing happened one Friday night at St. Mary's Hall. One of the songs we did was "Wipe Out," which has a drum solo. Gary, who was technically trained and could read notes, was without a doubt the best drummer Peter and I have ever played with. If Peter were here right now, he would back me up on that. Well, when Peter's lead came to an end in the song "Wipe Out," Gary's solo would start. On this occasion I looked at Pete, Pete looked at me and we shut off our amp. Don saw us and he shut his amp off and all of us proceeded to walk off the stage to go get pizza. You should have seen the look on Gary's face! I think he said something to us as we stepped off the stage. (And I'm positive it wasn't, "You guys are great.") Anyway, after about 15 or 20 minutes of Gary's drum solo we decided to go back up on stage and complete the song. Gary was about dead, covered in sweat, and ready to kill us. But all was forgiven and we would all laugh about it for years. We would continue to play school dances and St. Mary's Hall all through the year into 1967.

During the spring of 1967 we continued to play St. Mary's Hall and an occasional party. Peter and I both worked that summer, but we were cautious about spending our money. If we needed strings, sheet music or guitar equipment, we would buy it, but we didn't buy a lot of records. In a way we were all pretty lucky, because Don owned literally more than 100 albums that we could borrow. It was a good deal for Peter and me. That's how we learned most of our songs; by listening to them over and over on the record player.

Chapter Nine

It was Bazaar

In the summer of 1967, we had another of Don (the show boat) Jett's deals. Don's father worked for the State of New York, and the family of a guy he worked with owned a weekend/vacation resort in Highland, N.Y., across the river. This place had a full bar and dining room that entertained the adults. Their kids had a swimming pool, horseback riding and other activities during the day, but in the evening there were only a jukebox and pool table, so they decided to bring in a band for the kids.

The deal was we were to play on a particular Friday night and if they liked us, we could come back on the Sunday to play for their clam bake/barbecue. And if that worked out, we would be hired to play every weekend there once school ended throughout the whole summer, too, at $100.00 night. This was great! We thought we finally had made the big time. Well, we got there and there was a large room with a pool table, jukebox and tables and chairs. Through a doorway was a full bar on the other side of the wall. Things started out well; the kids were dancing and everyone seemed pleased with us. The lady that owned the place even made a big pizza for the band, and we had free Cokes; things were looking good.

That's right, you guessed it; something had to go wrong and it did. Don Jett, the bass player, was singing and playing, and he kept winking at a girl who was dancing. We didn't know this at the time, but she was 19 or 20 years old. The band members were all still in high school and, in fact, Peter was only 14, so we weren't supposed to be playing where alcoholic beverages were served. When it came time to take our break, Don started to walk outside so he could have a smoke. Well, waiting outside next to the doorway was the girl's 21-year-old boyfriend totally drunk. It seemed she'd had a fight with him that day and they had broken up. He grabbed Jett by a chain that Don always wore that had the letter "J" on it. The guy pulled Don to the sidewalk and started serving knuckle sandwiches to him. Just like in filmmaking, where a hand comes in to view with a clapperboard and you hear, "Action! Camera!" the entire place erupted into a brawl. I mean, there were fists being thrown, chairs and tables knocked over, and people yelling and screaming. It was unbelievable. None of us in the band had ever seen anything like this. We all ran for the car, and this crazed, drunken guy came after us, still trying to get to Don even after he'd gotten loose. We locked ourselves in the car. I remember this guy going around the car pounding on the windows wanting to get Don. Somebody called the N.Y.S. troopers, and the guy ran away and was hiding. But now all our equipment was inside and we didn't want to get out of the car.

What happened next was amazing. The rest of the kids gathered together all our stuff: Gary's drums and cymbals, our amps, the mikes. Pete and I had run out with our guitars at the beginning of the fight, we had worked hard to get them and we weren't about to leave them there to maybe get smashed or broken. The kids brought all our gear to the car, and other people kept an eye out for the guy. We packed our stuff and headed home. We got back to Bangall at about 1 or 2 in the morning. Farley, the lead singer, was young, and the poor guy was hyperventilating all the way home. After that experience, I don't remember Don Jett wearing that chain with the letter "J" hanging on it ever again.

In the summer of 1967, the church where Gary, Peter and I went, St. Anthony's, decided to put on a bazaar to raise money. Because we had been altar boys and Gary's parents were really involved with the church, we got the job to play at the Bazaar. No money, of course, because it was for the church, but we figured we would get a lot of exposure and they had let us use their basement to record our tape, so we thought we owed them. Well, the bazaar was a two-night event, Friday and Saturday. The band was positioned on a hay wagon and the place was packed. Unfortunately, everybody came over to listen to us play. Nobody was playing any of the games of chance that had been set up to raise money for the church. Finally some church fathers and Father John came over and asked us to stop playing for a while so the people would go and gamble away their money. It was funny at the time. My father only went to church at Christmas and Easter, and he was in charge of cooking the sausage and peppers for the bazaar. Even his sales were down. In spite of everything, I think the church made a lot of money. As you will see, this would later have consequences for our band.

When we went back to school in the fall of 1967, we picked up the last member of the band, Herb Robinson. He became our organ player. Herb was a genius; I remember he ordered a Heath Kit electronic organ and built it. We had to take it down to Vincitore's Piano store in Poughkeepsie to get it electronically tuned before he could use it.

We played the dances again, as well as St. Mary's Hall. Occasionally as a band we would go see other bands perform. Sometimes we would be inspired and other times depressed. There were a lot of good guitar players out there, but Peter and I kept practicing. We entered a couple of "Battle of the Bands" competitions. I think we came in second in one of them. In one of the competitions, I remember, Peter broke a string or strings on his 12-string guitar, and we didn't have time to replace them. The kid who had stolen the guitar from Robert Krause was playing in a band and he let Peter use his Fender Mustang for our next set, though he charged us $10.00 to use the guitar. Peter liked the guitar.

In the spring of 1968 Peter and I went to Kingston Music Store and traded in our knockoff Rickenbackers. I spotted a 1965 tangerine orange Stratocaster for $195.00, and I think Peter got a Fender Mustang like the one he borrowed. We kept these guitars for a number of years.

After playing together as a band for close to two years, artistic differences started to appear and there was some tension in the band. This came to a head the summer of 1968 when we played the church bazaar for a second time. It turned out to be our last engagement as The Sole Distributor. Don, Herb and Farley were bitching about not getting paid by the church while we knew they had made a lot of money the previous summer. Well, that got Gary's dander up. Peter and I sided with Gary, and that ended the band.

Chapter Ten
The Quiet, Busy Years

As we started the '68-'69 school year, Gary and I were seniors and both had steady girl friends. Peter was in 10th grade, and as I remember, he was interested in a girl named Suzie. We both played sports. Peter was a good baseball and basketball player. We were all doing our own thing at this point. Don, Farley and Herb hooked with up Mike Shockley from Standfordville and formed a band. Peter and I would still play our guitars together, but only in our room.

Laurel and I married in February 1969 and moved to Brockton, MA, six weeks after graduation with our 6-week-old daughter; Gary went off to college, and Peter graduated high school in 1971 and then went to college. I still had my Stratocaster but only played by myself. When we came back to New York in the spring of 1971, Laurel and I were expecting our second child, Peter was in college, and we were both pretty busy.

In the fall of that year while hunting geese with my brother Bill, my shotgun blew up. If it had blown up just a minute or two before it did, my brother Bill would either be dead or probably totally blind and in a vegetative state. It was that serious. His head had been just inches away from where the barrel split open and blew up. As it was, I lost the tip of my right pointer finger—the one that guitar players use to hold their pick. I thought my playing days were over.

As I remember it, months passed before I thought about playing again. It was sometime in 1973 that I started to play again, just using my thumb to strum. Peter introduced me to a group he liked called Creedance Clearwater Revival, and to a guy by the name of Jim Croce. Peter could always play Jim Croce well, especially "Time in a Bottle." We started playing with our folk guitars and do Jim Croce songs, not in public; just when we could get together. If it hadn't been for Peter's encouraging me to try to learn to strum again with a pick, I probably never would have played rock and roll electric guitar again. Peter and I went to Kingston Music Center and found some really long picks that I could use, and with practice, I got them to work for me. The gun accident had knocked me down, but I wasn't out and could play on.

In 1974 Peter and I started talking about forming another band. We talked to Gary and he was also interested. That was it; we were off and running again. All we needed was a bass player and some more equipment. Peter wasn't married yet. Gary had just gotten married, and I had a wife and two kids. So I did the only responsible thing to do: I went out and bought a huge amp and put it on my credit card. We went through quite a few bass players. One guy, Bruce Wallace, went by the name of "Far Out." He was a teacher, a hippie, and whatever else you could think of. But he was good. We would practice in our family's gas station on Sundays, and when we were done we would take Far Out to Millerton so he could take the bus to NYC where he substitute taught in Bedford Stuyvesant, a really bad area of the city. He had a Fender Jazz bass and an Earth amp. He would have his toothbrush and some clean underwear in his guitar case and that's all he traveled with!

Peter always loved the New York Yankees, and I remember one Sunday when we were practicing in the gas station the Yankee game came on in the middle of a song right through Peter's amp. It was unbelievable! Peter was stunned. We stopped playing and listened to the game awhile before it faded out. It must have been atmospheric skip or something. We all thought it was cool.

Chapter Eleven
Busted Out of Sour Apple Studio

Peter and I hadn't really done a lot of singing at that time, so we found a guy named Jimmy O'Sullivan, and he became the lead singer. We also picked up a keyboard player named Bob (Sherm) Couse. Far Out eventually left for greener pastures, and we found a really young kid named Spencer Robinson for our bass player. Spencer was probably 16, Gary and I were 23 and everybody else was in between. We practiced regularly but we weren't making any headway. Plus, it didn't help that the gas station wasn't a good place to practice. As a band, Peter, Jimmy, Bob, Spencer and I all chipped in and bought a Traynor PA System. We were serious about playing.

This next part of the story is absolutely true, and as I reminisce about it, I still can't believe the lengths we went to just to have a decent place to practice. One of the customers who came into the family's gas station was Oliver Adams who lived in Mount Ross, a little hamlet just outside of Pine Plains. Peter and I were talking with Mr. Adams one day and telling him about our band and how hard it was to find a good practice space. Mr. Adams mentioned that he had an old barn behind his house, and if we wanted to, we could look at it to see if it would work. The guys in the band were excited and we all went over on a Saturday to look at the barn. The barn was large enough, all right, but had no electricity and was filled up with rolls of canvas. (Mr. Adams had an awning business.) We were so desperate to find a place that we made a deal with Mr. Adams to rent for $100.00 a month, and we agreed to empty out the barn and fix it up so we could play.

We spent two weekends cleaning it out. We ran electricity from his house to the barn and wired the whole barn with outlets, put in neon lights, insulated the barn, and put plywood on the floor. Mr. Adams let us have the old rolls of canvas and so we completely covered the walls and ceiling with canvas and, to top it all off, I pulled the rug out of my living room and put it in the barn. The only guys left now besides me are Jimmy, Bob and Spencer, and if you asked anyone of them, they would tell you the acoustics were just like a sound studio; it was perfect! We were all flying high and thought we were on our way.

WRONG! We practiced in the barn exactly twice. The first time it was like magic; the sound was so good, I only had the volume control on my amp on 1 and Peter had his on 2 or 2-1/2 and everything sounded fantastic. Unfortunately the second time we played there, Mr. Adams got a complaint from his neighbor. Mr. Adams and his wife weren't complaining about the noise; in fact, they said they barely heard us, but his neighbor was complaining. So what do you do in a case like this? Well in the history of the world, this was probably the only time that the rock and roll band called the police. Yes, you read it right, we called the local police. They came and stationed an officer at the neighbor's house, one in Mr. Adam's house and one in the barn with us. We played a song and neither of the two officers in the houses thought we were too loud—they could hardly hear us. As we would find out later, the neighbor woman was going through the change of life and any little noise bothered her. Yet she worked right up the road at a saw mill where Jimmy and Bob worked and that noise didn't seem to bother her! Anyway, long story short, we didn't want Mr. Adams to have trouble with his neighbor, so we just walked away from everything, even after having spent a lot of time and money on that barn after just two practices. Now we were back to square one.

After that we practiced in the Pine Plains Lion Pavilion. Gary was a member, and made a deal that we could use it if we agreed to play at one of their functions. So that's what we did. Eventually we got a gig in 1975 at the high school for a dance. I found an old 8-track tape of that dance that my nephew Matt cleaned up and put on CDs. It's the only known recording of our second band, called "Busted Out." In a certain sense it was quite an appropriate name for us, given what we had been through to this point.

At another time, and I still don't know how this happened, somehow Gary got us a gig (or whatever!) right in the middle of his neighbor's daughter's wedding reception, who happened already to have a band booked. We played outside on the lawn at The Pines Bed & Breakfast while the "real" band was playing, under a tent; it was crazy.

After that things got hard again. Gary stopped playing. He was battling his own demons. Now we didn't have a drummer, so we started to advertise for one in the Pennysaver. Peter and I never really went in for loud rock and roll music, what some would call head-bangers stuff. We preferred what we called playing it clean, meaning using the least amount of added sounds. We did use a Fuzz box and later on a phase shifter, but that was about it. Some of the songs we played with Busted Out called for this type of enhancement, but Peter and I never got into heavy metal or any of the weird stuff. We also thought that we should be able to stand up in front of people and play the song at a sound level that made it sound like it was on the original record and to try to play to the size of the room. We didn't like playing too loud, and with some of our later drummers, the volume sometimes got out of hand. Then everybody seemed to go up in volume so they could hear themselves, including me, Peter, and the keyboard, and the next thing you knew, the lead singer had to scream and everybody else got hoarse. If you ever have a chance to listen to the CD of Busted Out at the Pine Plains High School dance, you'll hear how it got away from us a few times and you'll know what I mean about being too loud.

Around this time I started to take some lessons from a local guy named Frank Tamburrino, who had a band that played out regularly. He was an accordion player, and he taught me some scales and strums. He knew Gary and told us he could get us some work in Kingston if we could expand our repertoire to play some other kinds of music. We tried Hank Williams and some other country rock but most of the guys in the band didn't want to go in that direction. Peter and I liked the Beatles but the only song we ever did was Day Tripper.

Chapter Twelve
Always Trust Your Gut

Getting back to the problem of finding the right drummer, a kid from down in Pawling, N.Y., answered our advertisement. I remember he came up on a Sunday afternoon while we were practicing in the Pine Plains Sportsman Club. This was a block building with hardwood floors and was wide open. Our brothers, Bob and Bill, were club members and our father had been one of the original starting members. In fact he helped build it. Anyway, we somehow got the club to let us practice there for a small amount of rent. Well, the kid was pretty good though loud, and he seemed to have an attitude about him. I was leery but we needed a drummer if the band was going to continue.

The new drummer got us a job in Brewster at a Chamber of Commerce meeting/dance at a closed-down ski area. Then he got us a gig in Wappingers Falls for a kid's 18th birthday party at his home. That turned out to be kind of wild. The birthday boy ended up riding his motorcycle in the basement where we were playing. These younger guys had a little bit of a wild side to them. We all survived that.

I had purchased an old 1961 GMC panel truck that we used to go to and from our gigs. I remember the night we came home from the ski area gig, about 1 a.m. in the morning, As we were driving up Route 22 the truck started wrapping and banging. We didn't know if we would make it home. As it turned out, the bolts that hold the flywheel to the torque converter had loosened up and that's what was making the noise. It was quite an adventure that Saturday night.

When we started Busted Out we bought a lot of our equipment at Drome Sound in Albany, N.Y. Peter bought a brand new 25th anniversary Les Paul Gold Top guitar; it was beautiful. We also bought the PA, and I think Peter also bought a Fender Twin Reverb at the same time. I had my Strat and Monkey Ward's monster amp. We had come up a few steps up from those first electric guitars we had bought years earlier. As a band we all had pretty nice equipment now, the sound was good, and we had a place to practice, even though it was like playing in a thermos bottle (it definitely wasn't like the barn), and things were looking good.

Wrong again. This kid, the drummer, started to get on our nerves. Sometimes on Sunday he would cancel out on coming up to practice at the last minute. This was after everybody else was there. We even drove all the way to Pawling to pick him up a few times. It seemed like he was controlling the whole band. Our final gig as Busted Out came on a summer weekend in Pawling. The drummer had gotten us a chance to play for the Town of Pawling's "Pawling Day Celebration." We were to play on a 40-foot flatbed trailer in the town park. There were probably 1000 people there. It seemed ideal. We would play, and there were other groups and acts who would share the stage. We figured we could get a lot of exposure from it.

Well, we played our first set and that went well, then another act took the stage. Peter and I never liked leaving our guitars and amps unguarded (especially after Don Jett's experience with the drunken boyfriend all those many years ago). The drummer, lead singer and the bass player all left and went to the drummer's house somewhere in Pawling. Peter and I and, I think, Bob, stayed back to keep an eye on our equipment. When it was our turn to play again, we took the stage. I think we were playing "Hang on Sloopy." Well it soon became apparent that the drummer was having trouble holding the beat and the lead singer was forgetting the words to the song.

This is exactly what happened next. I looked at Peter, he looked at me, and we realized these guys were stoned. We gave each other the hand-sliding-across-the-throat sign, and that was it. Peter and I stopped playing right in the middle of the song, shut down our amps, unplugged our guitars and walked off the stage. That was the end of the band Busted Out. After that we sold the P.A. system and split the money. I remember selling my Strat (THAT was a mistake; it was pre-CBS!). Peter and I kind of just pulled back from playing. In our entire career from high school right to the end, Peter and I never smoked or did any kind of drugs. Gary and Don Jett used to smoke cigarettes. We all had the occasional beer, maybe some of us had more than they should have, but we never got into the other stuff. What happened down in Pawling was an affront to Peter and me. We vowed that it wouldn't happen again.

Chapter Thirteen
Heaven Came Down and Glory Filled Our Souls

The next few years brought a lot of changes for Peter and me; we found the true God. On a cold December night in 1975 there was a knock on our door. When I opened the door, there were two men from a local church. No, they weren't Jehovah Witnesses; they were members of a small, fundamentalist, Bible-believing church. The pastor was a classmate of Laurel's, and I had run track with him. His name is William Mayhew. He shared the gospel with my wife and me, and on January 8, 1976, we got saved.

My wife and I told Peter and Suzy about our conversion and they got saved a short time later. On February 26, 1976, Peter and Suzy came to know the Lord. We all started to attend Faith Bible Chapel in the little hamlet of Shekomeko.

As to our music, Peter and I would play together just for fun, usually Jim Croce tunes. At that time my only equipment was a Fender acoustic and my amp. My children were still very young and Peter and Suzy hadn't gotten married yet. Peter and Suzy had bought land and built a log cabin over the course of a number of years and in the fall of 1978, they got married.

In the spring of 1978, my wife and I moved to California with our kids. We were only there for six months, and moved back a few weeks after Peter and Suzy were married. It seems like I always missed the big events in Peter's life. For me there's a certain sadness about that, but I can't change those things now.

During the years we attended that church, we met a couple of brothers, Al and Leroy Stevenson. They were both guitar players. They were originally from Western Pennsylvania. They did a lot of picking and had what Pete and I would call a mountain music style. We used to stay after services on Sundays at the Chapel and play together. Peter and I were getting back to our roots in acoustic folk music. We started to play some of the songs that were in the hymnal. I even wrote a couple of Christian songs that are still in my acoustic guitar case.

Peter and me practicing our church songs

On March 26, 1982, Peter and I purchased two brand-new Applause electric acoustic guitars from Kingston Music Center. The total cost was $560.70 for both. In fact, I still have that receipt in my guitar case. For anybody who knows the Bart boys, we don't like throwing anything away. Our wives can attest to that! (Ok, enough of that.) Moving right along, Peter and I played with these two guitars for a number of years.

In April of 1982, Peter and I were practicing some songs from the hymnal that we were going to play at church the next Sunday. We were in Peter's living room in their log cabin. Peter had one of those small cassette tape recorders. When we finished practicing, we decided to record the songs to see how they sounded. At the last minute, after we had recorded the hymns, I told Peter about a song I was working on but still had only one verse. I played it for him. Then Peter told me just to play the chords and he would try to put some melody on top them. That song is "Gonna Love You Til the End." I don't know why things happen like that, but that was the only recording of this song and the only time Peter and I ever played it. After Peter passed away, I asked my nephew Matthew, Peter's son, to see if he could do anything with the original tape recording. What you hear today is the result of what Matt did with it. It is pretty amazing, especially if you get to hear the original tape.

In May, 2018, I sent the song in to get a copyright from the Library of Congress and received it in December 2018. I want the world to remember Peter and me. Especially Peter, since if it hadn't been for his lead guitar, it would still be just another song in my guitar case. I used to joke with Pete and say that we were the second best rock and roll lead and rhythm guitar combo in the world. And Peter would say, "Second?" and I would say everyone else is tied for first place. Peter would chuckle.

We played that Sunday in front of the church. Unfortunately, old habits die hard and some of the songs came out a little bit sounding like doo wop or rock and roll. We got some stink-eye looks and some disapproving head nods. So after that, Peter and I just continued to practice and play together whenever we could.

As the years rolled by, my kids were growing up and in 1987 our daughter graduated and went off to college. In 1989, our son graduated from high school and joined the Army. Peter and Suzy's children were still quite young, and I remember Peter telling me about a group called "Beatlemania." We went to listen to them a couple of times and that was it; we were ready to play real rock and roll again. This time, The Sole Distributor was going to play the Beatles.

Chapter Fourteen
Last Train Out of the Station

Peter and I decided that if we were going to play Beatles music, we wanted to sound like them. In 1990 I bought my last guitar, a Rickenbacker 325 John Lennon model with a 3/4 neck. It was over a thousand dollars, by far the most I had ever spent on a guitar. Peter had a solid body mahogany Les Paul and a thin body Epiphone. Peter had sold my Montgomery Ward amp for me back in 1978, so I needed another amp. Pete and I decided to buy two brand-new Fender 80 Chorus amps; we still have them today. I also bought a brand new Peavey P.A. system with Cobra monitors. Pete and I made stands for the column speakers. We even made amp stands. I made mine out of muffler pipe. (I had a pipe bender at my service station and I bent the amp stand out of pipes.) I still have that stand today. As of the writing of this story, I gave Matthew the P.A. system to keep everything in the family.

In the early 90s Peter and I went to a local lady, Norma Midthun, for singing lessons. She was a retired music/voice teacher in our town. We wanted to see if she could help us find out what would be the best keys for us to sing in. After all, in this our last band, it was going to be Pete and me doing all of the singing. I remember she gave us our ranges and good keys to sing in. That's why if you look into our music collection, you'll find some songs re-marked two or three times in different keys.

Gary came on board one more time. He went out and bought a brand new set of Sonar drums. They were black, beautiful, and made in Germany. They were really nice and very expensive. We weren't holding back on anything. Peter was taking guitar lessons from a fellow in Milan named Steve Gravino, who was really, really good. We still needed a bass player and auditioned a few guys. Eventually a young kid named Dave Brooks who was also taking lessons from Steve became our final bass player. Prior to that, a local fellow named Rick Meryman practiced with us a number of times. He played keyboard and guitar.

One of the best things about the last band was that we actually had a good place to practice. Peter had built a three-car garage next to his log cabin. It was heated and insulated, and we could leave some of the equipment there. This proved to be a godsend. We used a whole bay of the garage to play in. Gary could leave his drums there; I left the P.A. system. It was as if we had our own Apple Studio. For quite some time we would practice at least two or three times a week. Peter's wife, Suzy, is an excellent baker and she would always make us cakes or pies which we would have during practice. Sometimes I think we just came for the desserts. (Just kidding!)

As I write this through my tears, I remember these happy times. I remember Rina (Peter's little girl) standing on a stool next to me, singing "Hang on Sloopy" into the microphone, and Matt on the drums. You just don't forget moments like that. I remember Matt, who has always been good with electronic stuff, taping us a number of times. Before Dave Brooks came into the band, there was a fellow who was from Millerton, named Bruce, who played bass. He can be seen on some of the YouTube videos that Matt's posted. One of the videos was at the Pine Plains Lions Club. It was Peter, Gary, Bruce and me as The Sole Distributor.

The times I'll always remember

During the summer of 1994 I remember practicing up at Peter's and when we took a break and went outside, we could faintly hear the music from the Woodstock Reunion which was going on across the river. I remember we could see the glow in the skyline from all the lights, and you could just barely hear the sound of the bass music across the valley; it was amazing.

As I've said earlier, we practiced a lot. We got some gigs at home parties, we played at a wedding in Western Mass in Stockbridge, near Great Barrington, in the mountains, and we played in Bangall again, which I thought was kind of ironic. This time instead of playing at St Mary's Hall as we had done 30 years earlier, we played a restaurant/bar called Stage Stop, about a quarter of a mile away. I guess we had come full circle, thought now Don Jett, Farley Churton and Herb Robinson weren't with us.

Our final gig as a band was in the summer of 2003. Gary's wife, Jo Ann, worked at the Pine Plains Post Office and one of the rural mail carriers, a lady named Terry, was the representative for the postal union employees. They were having a state convention down in Fishkill, N.Y., and they needed a band to play one of the nights. We played for just two hours after their dinner and we got paid really well. It was the most any of us had ever been paid to play. After that, we started to drift apart:

Gary didn't want to play, I was in the process of getting ready to move to Maine, and Peter was already involved with The Gospel Truth, the a cappella group he, Matthew our brother-in-law, Doug, and friend George Frick, were forming. The last song that I ever played with my little brother, Peter, was "For Your Love" by the Yardbirds. I remember it as if it was yesterday. You can hear us play it on some of our YouTube videos. We always had trouble with some of the high notes, but we always gave it our best shot.

Chapter Fifteen
Road Trip!

"A cup of coffee and a piece of pie." That's what Peter and I would say to each other after we had been out looking at guitars and amps. Whenever we went to Kingston or Poughkeepsie to music stores to look at equipment, Peter and I would try to find a diner and have a cup of coffee and a piece of pie. I know this doesn't sound like much, but it was something we did, and we always talked about music, the Beatles, equipment; it was our little quirky thing that we shared.

On a Saturday in February, sometime in the early '90s, Pete and I took a road trip. A chemicals vendor who came into my garage found out that Pete and I had a band. He mentioned that his father-in-law was a music teacher and that he had a lot of equipment for sale. As it turned out, he lived in Roscoe, N.Y., in a big three-story Victorian house and his place was filled to the rafters with musical instruments. I think the guy had 600 Suzuki violins out on rental! Anyway, Pete and I drove up there that Saturday in my '74 Pontiac station wagon. We came home with a Rickenbacker 4000 bass, a 1970 Fender Telecaster Custom, a Fender Jaguar "Green Label," a Guild single pickup blond thin-line hollow body and a Kay stand-up bass. Quite the haul! The Fender Jaguar turned out to be a fake, but the guy gave us our money back on that. I think Peter and I doubled or tripled our money on the items we sold, so we made out well. I guess you could say we were the early "American Pickers." That was just one of the many little jaunts Pete and I took over the years. I look back fondly on these times. They are happy memories of the little things that Pete and I did together, and I will always cherish them.

From the summer of 2003 to about November or December of that year, I played with my nephew John, Dave, and a drummer named Jeff Hall. We would practice up at John's garage. Jeff was a good drummer but different in style from Gary. John was very studious. He was willing to learn any songs. At the time I was having trouble with my breathing and coughed a lot so I couldn't sing very well. We were also getting ready to move, so that was the final chapter of my musical journey. I have not played with anyone in a band since moving to Maine in February 2004.

Chapter Sixteen
The Long Goodbye

Fast forward to February 2018. I came home from my job one evening to find that my brother, Bill, had called. The message was about Peter. He had had a medical emergency and had been rushed into surgery. It turned out that he had a stage 4 glioblastoma brain tumor that was malignant. The day after the surgery he suffered what the doctor's called a "bleeder." He had emergency surgery, but too much damage had been done. He had to be put in a coma to keep him calm. That night I drove all night to Pine Plains. I got to Bill and Dawn's house around 3:00 in the morning.

The next day we went to the hospital to see Peter. It was really hard on me to see Peter just lying there. I remember that they had a radio up next to his bed with the local classic rock station playing. I guess they hoped this might help him to come out of the coma. As I looked at Peter I remembered calling him a few weeks prior on his birthday, January 17th. He had just turned 65. We talked about the kids and everyday stuff. He'd just signed up for Medicare, and he mentioned that his eyes were bothering him some and that he sometimes had trouble with his words. I don't know how long this had been going on, but these are both signs of some kind of neurological problem. One thing that gives me some solace is that before I hung up with Peter that night, I told him I loved him. Those were the last words he would ever hear from me.

The doctors said that if he didn't come out of the coma, they couldn't treat his cancer and that because of the damage from the bleeder, he probably wouldn't live more than a year or so. They couldn't get all of the tumor and it was a rapidly growing type. The decision to put Peter in hospice care was made: now it was just a waiting game. As Peter lay there, he occasionally moved his arms or hands. The doctors thought he could probably hear us. His eyes would twitch if you talked to him; but other than that, there was no communication. I put my hand on Peter's and it was warm. His hands were much larger than mine. My mind went back to the time I had purchased my Rickenbacker and how Peter tried to play it and how he mentioned that the neck of the guitar was too narrow for his fingers. When I pressed my hand against his, I was hoping he could transfer some of the talent in his hands to mine. During all the years we played together, all the hours we practiced, Peter's hands were like a glove covering my hands, making me sound good when we played together. Now it was all coming to an end.

The last known "The Sole Distributor"
business card, now with Peter
in his final resting place

I had written a song back in 1993 when our mother died. I called it "Rosie." I had kept that song to myself all those years. I could never sing it all the way through without crying. I always thought maybe Peter could sing it, but now it was too late. I know now I must move on. I play my guitar on Sunday mornings by myself, just like I used to do. Only now I look up at my photograph of Peter and try to imagine him standing next to me playing his leads. That's all I have now—memories and recordings and videos. I hope that's enough. I know someday when my heart beats its last beat and I take my final breath and the light is no longer in my eyes, I will go through that door called death to the other side. And I know one of the first voices I'll hear will be Peter's. I can hear him now saying, "Hey, Chuck, how's it going? I've been waiting for you. You're gonna love this place! We all have perfect bodies, everyone has perfect singing voices, and there aren't any 'Mack Truck' guitars" here, they all play real easy." Then he'll say, "I found Gary and Jett. Let's play!" And I'll say, "Great! What do you want to play?" And they will say in unison, "Let's start with

GLORIA!"

And that, ladies and gentlemen, is how I envision what is going to happen. Two brothers who started out in a sheep shed will be with the Lamb of God.

May God bless my little brother, Peter
Rest in peace

Acknowledgements

My profound and sincere thanks to:

Charlotte and George Draper's editing suggestions and encouragement;

Matthew Bartolomeo for his photos and photo editing contributions;

Jo Ann Keeler for the photos she took at St. Anthony's;

Herbie Robinson for sharing his Sole Distributor photos;

My wife, Laurel, for typing my handwritten draft and formatting it for publication;

Everyone who shared their stories of Peter and our bands and helped bring back the memories.

Appendix

Charlie and Peter talking about Sole Distributor:
https://www.youtube.com/watch?v=uD6iYUW0TRM&feature=yout
u.be&fbclid=IwAR2lqBMyYdhI_gPSbrXKX42nVQIoAGspXLTKtF
0Sm1sFrwNsOpQYEwf7s3A

Sole Distributor "My Only Dreams"
https://soundcloud.com/user-270590964/sole-distributor-my-only-
dreams?fbclid=IwAR1auGtSgmuVvEEgQtS7HYN7-
w2ugFaGStC79IBo_d-EqWevbup9cB564_w

7/27/94 "Sleep Walk" at the Pine Plains Lions Club

https://www.youtube.com/watch?v=ED9lkLCWnJE&feature=youtu.

be&fbclid=IwAR0Zr56BHbnT6P693FAHJHyJfdvi6t4k0d5jY8lUC6N

v6Su8Up5i51GhTzE

"Walk Don't Run" at the Pine Plains Lions Club

https://www.youtube.com/watch?v=yQbPaAKsG7k&feature=youtu.

be&fbclid=IwAR17hgae9cYfVwyAsHb0JlWicHLVUy7U5VYoerBFh

w--rtdUqx-chqUKcww

Made in the USA
Middletown, DE
24 August 2019